19 Poems
&
7 Quotes

Sara Jessimy Kruzan

Copyright © 2018 Sara Kruzan

All rights reserved.

ISBN: 978-1-7268-0175-1

DEDICATION

19 poems and 7 quotes are a work of personal thoughts, feelings, experiences, and reflections through a poetic expression rooted from years of integration.

This book of expression is dedicated to the women especially who welcomed me, spoke into my life while incarcerated. I am a reflection of you all!. Anita Ford, you know you wrapped me up in your arms with such available motherly love! Thank You ever so! Laverne DeJohnette, Man! You always was a cheer leader for Sahara! Told You you would come home!!!! Chubby!!!! Always be my soul sister you are a true friend and we got this !!!! Gonna bring you home!!! Tabatha Brown, we have been best friends since I was 18, you 23, hey remember when they put all of us brand new baby lifers in the same room!!! Remember when...nah I will save that for later!!! Let's just say our mattresses were plush ...for a very short time! Gina Jeans, so happy you are home! You tricked me though in CYA, you know that wasn't right! Glad you are living your best life girl!!! Niki, thank you for sharing years of friendship! Wish you all the best girl Freedom is around the corner!

Amy Davis! Speaking your truth inspires many! You'll be home soon!! Michelle, seeing you in the yard tending to the beauty of nature inspired me, watching you do your time as an LWOP sculpted me in many ways! Lupita...girl we are soul sisters!!! Classy, Dana-butt, Cheryl Face, Ms. Bea, Michelle...we all out what happened to our Christmas in Hawaii, let us not blame it on the volcanoes we have all endured more than that! Smile!! Erica, may you have such peace inside girl you next for this freedom train! KiKi...not ever will you be left behind or forgotten. Stranger, always having a holiday sale or holiday bags for us! You give such joy!! Momma Gwenn! My one and only fairy God-mother, you are the epitome of strength! Sheryl...your smile and kindness tickle my soul and heart to this day! Thank you! Tess, hummingbird spirit, you gave me so much on the friendship side!! Tyra, can you believe it!!!! Boxer, Blanca hugs to your soul! Deepest Gratitude to everyone who pulled together to bring me home!! I am who I am today because of All of You!!! Summer Reign Justice, may you always chase the sun, run with the rainbows, plant seeds which will bring forth life and know you are my hope in the flesh!

CONTENTS

Acknowledgments	i
1st Quote	1
Friendship	2
Haunted Shadows	4
2nd Quote	7
The Obnoxious Ego	8
Dick Slangin' Yo Dick	17
Painfilled Wombs	19
3rd Quote	22
Metal Bunk Beds	24
My Fears	28

4th Quote	31
Stone into Wood	32
Concrete Wall	34
5th Quote	35
Poverty Pimps	37
Dirty Water	41
6th Quote	43
I Know What the Devil Looks Like	45
7th Quote	49
Free From Within	50
Polysyndeton and Word Porn	51

Still Soul, Steal Soul, Steel Soul	52
NIMBY x3	53
Just Write	56
Roots	58
Woods Glass Lamp	62

ACKNOWLEDGMENTS

Simply when we are made aware to do better…we must do better. I accept a truth of incarceration infused with any type of violence is not ever a healthy approach to healing. We all have a birth right to freedoms!, joy and purpose filled opportunity.
Acknowledging the power of Love!

1st Quote

"Be gentle with yourself, flexible and remember we as humans reflect off one another"

Sara J Kruzan

FRIENDSHIP

Feeling free to Be!

Recall of moments created with ease and comfort

Individuals who are an extended version of our truest self

Eventually we may disagree

Dancing...random moments of glee

Simple smiles spreading wild

How will this get better

I listen and apply

Purpose is developed in a friendship between

You and I

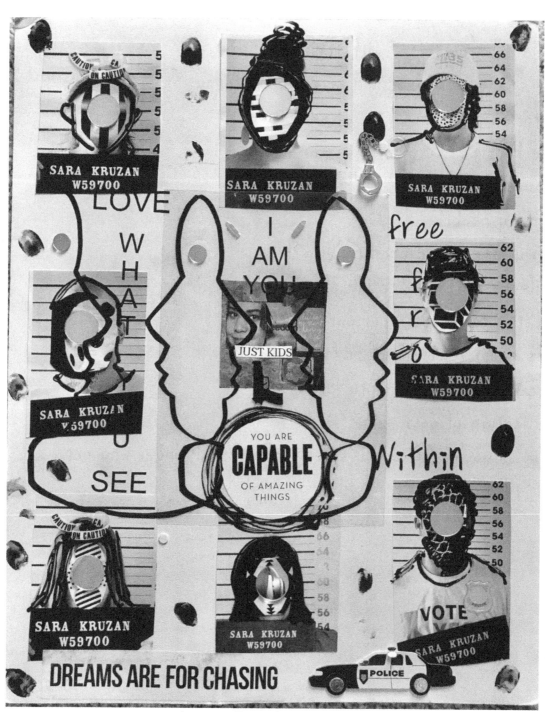

Photo collage by SJK 2018

Haunted shadows

Head held down contorted with their pain
Another strangers Dick assaulting my body today
Unable to ask for help –
Not sure how to
Too many oversights
Engaging my plight!
Dick in my face forced upon my mouth
Sweet silence discovered inside of myself
How sad it is to witness your own decay
And he's so far removed so far far away
Dick forced against my squinty face
Oh, the torture of your pain
Wait I'm 11 you're 48 and it's not really rape Wonder why not
So, I'm Still a slave?

Art work by SJK 2018

2ND QUOTE

"Let not the traumas experienced, define or redefine your purest truth"

Sara Jessimy Kruzan

The Obnoxious Ego

I need for you to hear me

See me smell me and Oh yeah...

feel

me
Validate me, for look @

I...

am so
Great!

In fact, I've so much more to say
Please wait

Where are you going?
  Why you leave?

don't you always wanna listen about me

know me see me?
what about this···
come on
come absorb me
do you not know who I am
I mean
LOOK At ME ;)
Do you not google search me?
Invading my public privacy?

I have a plethora of labels,
degrees

that **TOTALLY**

highlight
me

Oh yeah and of course

look at me

I speak with ego most of the time
telling you about all my great works in my life...

Hey!

hello do you hear me?

I just won an award,

legendary you see I know because Someone else validated me through their value placement of what

a real HerO is to be!

You need to pay me at least 100 plus geez

I mean come on. Isn't that what most

men did to me?

it's all really about me

and I know this to be!

if it wasn't for I

you know that placating We,

iS a Sleep

Wake up!

It's still All about me!

please read the fine print to see that the first letter in

We

is simply

A W that's asleep!

wak**e** up,

stand up...

Ah see its still about <u>M</u>e!

Hey! I need for you to hear me!

See Me!

Oh yeah feel me!!

You Must Validate Me!

Art work by SJK 2018

Dick Slangin yo' Dick

Why you gotta be doing all this? Your Dick slangin has imprinted the following within my cells...

D is for: Demanding... Devour... Demeaning... Dehumanizing... Damn... Disgusting... Damaging... Dollars... Dissolving... Degrading... Distinguished...Dumbass... Damp... Dirty... Dildo... Doggish... Detrimental... Death... Don't...Deliberate...Desperate...Disposable...

I is for: Individual...Ickier...Ice... Injects...Injures...Injurer...Implant... Inconsistent...Isolated...Isolation...Idolized...Instant...Inquisitive... Invasive...Insatiable...Irresponsible...Irregular...Implode

C is for: Careless...Caution...Cautious...Contagious...Careful...Carefree...Coarse Course...Cunning...Curious...Consideration...Children...Cold...Core... Compared...Contemplative...Curse...Callous...Cancer...Cell...Cellblock

K is for: Karma... Knock...Knocked-up... Knowledge... Knowledgeability... Knack...Ker plunking...King Cobra...Ka...Ketosteroid...Knotty

Can you please really think about what you wish to deposit in the lives of others? For this approach has caused layered harm and trauma...

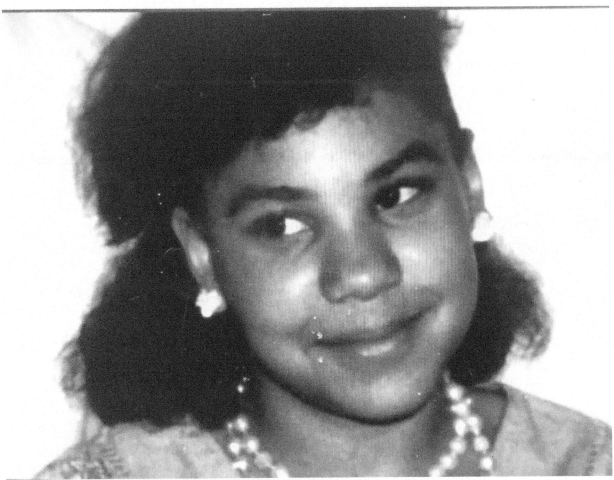
SARA KRUZAN 1988

Painfilled Womb

We fight the plight within the womb
    Unbeknownst to you
        the delicate formation
            which takes place
                within invisible space
                    this sacred place

where life begins and ends
    I won despite the odds
        of 1 in 100 Milli-On
            and yet because of your pain
                you wished me away

for $200 of a debt society dolla
 to this day we all pay
    and somehow
        someway
            our presence is now

yet my soul

and heart feel
 so betrayed
  my soul says
   it'll be OK
why do you look at me with such enraged hate?
   it's not my fault
 wasn't the one who did this to you
    exposed are your pained fumes

    please do not
     in your rage
      take it out on me

  just simply hold me
 learn to love me

   I'm not him
    I'm not his lack of love
     and compassion
      I'm a gift of life
       I'm your beautiful distraction
      I know your roots
        feel so betrayed
         and yet my soul can say
          sweet one...

it'll be OK.
   these are my thoughts
      from the soul of my life's
         first day.

3rd Quote

"We are not only the reflection of humanity – we are the very echo etched within the wind"

Sara Jessimy Kruzan

Art work by SJK 2018

Metal Bunk bed

My assigned bunk bed awaited my arrival
cold quiet
yet loud with institutionalized structural suffocation
and survival
bunk bed
what am I to do with you
I prefer the lower bunk even though
I'll begin to fold into myself
another form of an oppressive death
and yet I'm the one with a life sentence?
death sentence, a death sentence
a bit too late
for bunk bed
you are truly
a metal coffins
absorbing the death in which arrived
along my side
in this cold and sterile metal gate
no one really showed up for the funerals except a tear
of 4 plus 4 more equals 8
all done!
it's unlock

gotta go
such a rush
snap mugshot
all around!!
zipping
zapping
despising
mental
emotionally
socially constructed
trapping
metal death bed
where do you put the pain?
in a metal sterile box?
Unlock!
Gotta go…
not sure how this all works
you know

the encapsulating
of the pain
Payne
PAYNE housing staff name
Ever you remember
A reminder everyday
of what we experience
as we fall asleep
upon and within our metal death beds

Kruzan W-59700 2013 Central California Women's Facility

My fears

my fear is not of surviving
My fear is of pathetically dying
My spirit is not to be broken
my spirit is to be constantly hoping
for a miracle
A chance
in another time
young feet must dance
bright eye smile
confident walk of prison blue attire style
ha ha some may laugh
it can be an uncomfortable funny
life without parole...
a very long while
fantasies and dreams swallow you whole
it's so painful to have a hole in your soul amusement
engulfs empty silence
cold air inspires to find
extreme pleasure in such simple dares
you question
The time

the place
and the where's...
it's just you and me
me and you
that is me
I am the 2
simple complex
calm or a wreck I have a dream
like that man Mr. King you see
it is to be completely free!

Sara enjoying the moment 2018

4th Quote

"In painting, creating, dancing and being life explodes and expands"

Sara Jessimy Kruzan

STONE INTO WOOD

Born on an ancient track
expose the nail send magic back
Awake, embrace. Retell Your story
Face to Face, Impart the Glory
Sara you've got stars in your eyes
Paint on your wings, rainbows that fly.

Sara you don't care what they say
Fight your own battle, pave your own way.
You drink the milk of paradise
Pouring out old wounded cries

All that's best of dark and light
Shines inside your heart and Eyes
Walk ahead with Kings and Queens
Beyond the walls of crime.

Shadows of eternity
Rich in the spoils of time.
Sara you've got dreams that are real
Fragments of world's made from all little girls.
Sara, you turn bad into good…
Red into silver,
Stone into Wood.

Sara Kruzan and Juvenile hall counselor Hickman 1995 High school Graduation

Concrete Wall

My wall so beautiful delicate and sleek
my wall so harsh so cold you run so deep
deep into not only my mind
my soul my body my present time
let it go
but no no no more tears
I wish would not fall
but here I lay forehead touching my concrete wall
we've been so close from the first day
here we are 19 years later 7 months and 2 days
you know my every little thing from despair to joy
to faith
and hoping
wishing
death to end it all
this feeling of pain
I don't want to cope
and all my dreams that were once a distant hope
beautiful while you stand so tall
I thank you for all you saw
we believed
for now, I must go
physically free
for the State says I can be
I beam as I leave
thank you steel beast
as I met you I meant me
my wall so beautiful delicate and sleek
my wall so hard so cold ...runs so deep
deep into not only my mind my soul and my body
time to go
no more tears I wish would not fall
here I lay forehead touching
Ever present wet concrete wall

5th Quote

"Looking into the eyes of others without judgment forgiveness comes with a recognizable ease"

Sara Jessimy Kruzan

visual story telling by SJK

Poverty Pimps:

The definition of exploitation is as follows, thank you Webster all credit to you!

number one, a noun:
the action or fact of treating someone unfairly to benefit from their work

number 2 noun:
the action of making use of and benefiting from resources

Hey poverty pimp is you a self-selected front-runner of the deprived you know the us who are deemed as sectional?

Do you take great smugness in eulogizing the continuous poorness of one's ethnicity?

Are you quite well-off stanching from their efforts to inspire a share at the cocktail conversations?

Do you work at the drop of a cap to have a frontal face spontaneous snap, audio conversationalist alongside a Hollywood advertisement?

Are you usin" white guilt to gain credibility, money and influence?

Are you aware of the true definition of the word Racist?

Hey poverty pimps with way too many faces...

Are you a social worker a do-good Director of a nonprofit organization who only steps into the hood under the protection of corrections observation?

Are you still on the plantation?

White Knight wez don't need savin!

What wez need is for you to please stop
pre-ten-ding
and really look at your behavior...
because it's kinda really you know you who keeps us on the bus.

I guess it's because we fought so hard to be on one and in the front in the first place.

                We had ambition that's for sure!

Interesting how that bus
    took Us
        to laborious
          jobs
that paid pennies to simply make life easier for those outside of our us...

  That Bus!

    That Bus drove us
      to the enslavement within the big un-red zone approved homes
        you know the one the banks of the Freeland make sure we can't live in and own
          all about that zip code!

      maybe it's because we aren't physically free
      simply re-owned.

What's that number of the amendment?

Oh yeah 13th,
which clearly reads:

neither slavery nor involuntary servitude except as a punishment for a crime where of the party shall have been duly convicted shall exist within the **untied** states or any place subject to their jurisdiction

 oops,

please **pardon** me!

somehow in the read

that "**it** factor" was rearranged...

Strange Same thing happened to the slave.

Sara Jessimy Kruzan

ART BY SJK 2018

Dirty Water

Rooted on the floor

I looked around

Wall bare

to recreate

and there you left me once again

purest core of my soul

you left me again

beautifully crafted

creating a forward motion

metal bed full of pain

how many faces

you held each fear

metal bed metal head

What fear and trauma imprinted in your cells

Cellblock

Tear

metal bed metal head

with trauma rooted in

of it's going to get better

your sins I've conquered

open and pure

all your hats down

Only New space

the beauty of the unknown

this time I'm smiling from the

blank white pure wall

intricate soul

each moment of the now

of discovery to an unknown

oh

and hearts can you name

carried and absorb my darkest loneliest tear

metal flying past your ears

Cells

Tier

All rooted in fear...

decades later we put you together

unrealistic fantasies

untruth

you throw dirt on me under the purest skies of blue

common truth

metal head

unlock ...

time to heal and let go

each intentional twist to unlock

for removing that dirt of ancestral trauma

fruit so rotten,

connecting

you and I

nor I so low

know

to the left we release

we go against the grain

reign

what a gift from the universe

pure whitewall

left again from generations of unheard and embrace debaucheries

is to not resist

for the pure canvas father

of your dirty water

my mother's too

blue brings healing

in gratitude metal bed

decades later

again...

metal bed metal bed

please and thank you

unpleasant fruit

generationally recycled in the cotton

connected

you no better

and so, with that

in lightning failings of the twist to unlock

we make a modification

we make our souls rain

REIGN with healing

through you

smile in my soul

the gift of closing the pain

yet embrace

is the complete opposite

6ᵗʰ Quote:

"When you stop chasing the sun you wilt away"

Sara Jessimy Kruzan

Visual art by SJK 2018

I know what the devil looks like

It's cold
I'm cold,
Shivers assault my bones
Raining…skirt wet,
Hair damp and heavy,
Heavy like my heart,
Forget what it's like to look up
Ever too familiar with the repetition seen in the concrete walk-
Sloshing of wet tires echo within my ears,
The awkward click, clack of the heels was made to wear
Reminds me of what lies ahead

A dirty bed,
Full of prior deposits,
An empty grumble from somebody's husband
The devil speaks sometimes sings in between the hotel, motel sheets-
Cum on the pillows,
Cum on my face-
Cum from a stranger-
Emptied waste,
The very sight of uncooked eggs makes me ache
Reflux is a gag

Wanted to be a doctor,
Once had dreams and goals,
The intelligence to achieve it, yet…instead my body was sold.
Doctors did however show up in my life
Just on this course, it was
Their PHD dick in which they paid with our American Debt dollar… to assault me and thrust into my mouth.

Over sexualized at the age of nine
…molested…raped…by the age of 11
School was an outlet until they raped me…
Summer vacation-
No one around…three gang members is how I was found…

At the same school that
once held promise
Three guys violence,
Which rearranged my hypothalamus
Something changed that day June 1991

"Hey" a voice with shame filled testosterone infused anticipation speaks out...
"Pssst, hey...You...ah! You ready for a good time?"
His red hair still haunts me to this day...
Off duty officer for the LA P Die
Deep sigh
I must follow the rules,
No kissing, no long talk, just please and move...
No words can escape my mouth
After all I am too busy preparing for the paid rape, if only I could shout...
But I can't

Because something happened to me back in June 1991...
That promise that broke my hypothalamus-
Rain drops, pubic on a weathered napkin-
Exposed and given as a trust offering,
I close my eyes, my heart and soul protected...
Penis in my mouth-
This community so broken and infected
Something died...
Many of times...
The healing component-
The tenacity to strive to be resurrected.
Car door slams...
Heels assault my senses...
It's cold,
Shivers assault my bones...

Raining,
Skirt wet
Hair damp and heavy
Heavy like my heart,
Heavier now than a while ago...
Forgot what it's like to look up
Ever too familiar with the repetition seen in the concrete walk
Sloshing of wet tires echo within my ears,
The awkward click,
Clack of the heels
Hells I was made to wear
Is my skirt tight enough?
Re-apply the rouge
Gently run my fingers around the curve of my ears which now secures my damper hair,

"Hey"
That familiar urge to seek and find
Tag I'm it
Now is the time
Hey, yes yes you!
His words ooze with perverted glue-

I look at his face-
Looks so clean and nice-
However, I know that's exactly what
The devil looks like.

I am just 13
With a rearranged loveless Life

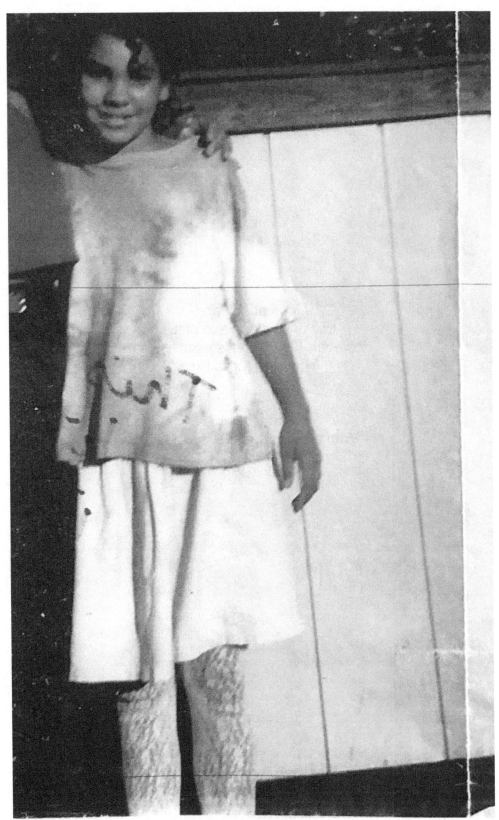

Sara in the 6th grade

7th Quote

"Life starts with water, water molecules create harmony, in harmony…fluidity"

Sara Jessimy Kruzan

Free from within

You
are more than enough
Your smile
Your eyes
That beautiful skin
Sweet curious soul
You are free from within
Dance with love
Fearless ness
Reach
for the grand of the land
Look around
All the others you see
They too are kin
Kin-dred spirits having
The present experience
It's all about the free
From within
Liberate yourself
No one owns you!
Awaken the warrior
All women and all men
Awaken and Rise!
For you are free from within
Your soul speaks through the eyes
Our words
Intentions
Surrenders
You are seen
You will win!
Remember with each movement forward
It must start within

Polysyndeton and Word Porn

Sex	and		
Fun	and		
Lost	and	in	uncertainty
Pretend	love	see	pain
And	fucked	**open**	and
and	**Shamed**	and	eyes
and	do it	forward	fall
again	and	free	**and**
dance	and	and	be
be free	and	and	dance
fall	forward	do it	**again**
and	eyes	shamed	and
and	**open**	Love	fucked
and	see	and	pretend
and	the	lost	and
pain	in	fun	and
uncertainty	and	sex	

Still Soul   Steal Soul   Steel Soul

Simply
Testing
Individuality
Liken
Love
Simply
Open
Understanding
Lonely
Spaces
Telling
Easy
Accusations
Lessons
Seen
On
Undercover
Lens
Soul searching
Tempted
Elation
Eclectic
Limitations
Simply Still
Openly
Understanding
Lonely

NIMBY x3

Not	Never	No Way!
In	Intended	I will Allow
My	May You	Messes Like You
Back	Be Free to Choose	Believe
Yard	You Know	You Have Value

Is the Nimbyx3 the new obvious, intentional segregation model for the present moment?

Listening to Ear Hustle 2018

Just Write

Write Your Life, write it all out!
Create what you believe
you deserve
want
and need
No one can write your life
Unless
you allow them
the space
to hold.
Beautiful soul- you are heard
Seen, accepted and ever so deserving
Far worth more than tangible items, platinum, gold...
Write and Create all you wish to Be!

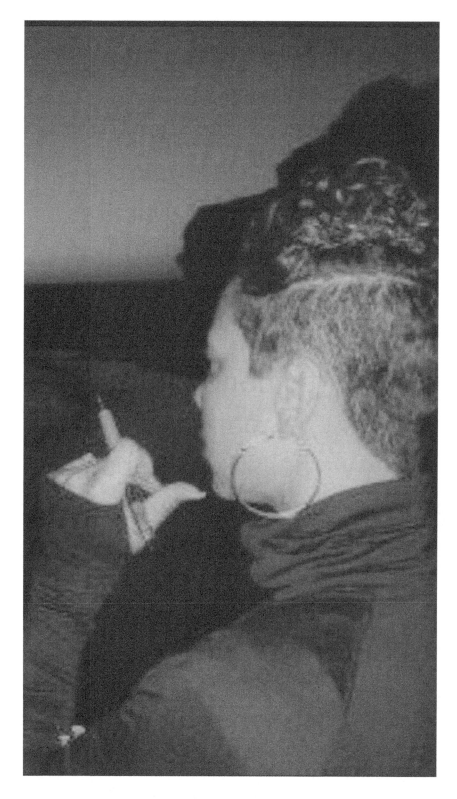

Sara Kruzan 2013 Laguna Beach California

Roots

Lyrical composure
creates and complicates
Exhaustive realizations
Manipulations,
ego driven intentions
tired bone aching
pain
Verbal stipulations
Barking orders to oppress one's natural right
Shower compassion upon the seeds planted in
the night
Desolate in need of a drink
mud
Unhealed civil wars
A need?
Blood
fostered growth
Civil wars

no more
Intricate in detail
Unseen and heard
Torn from mourn
Yet crying so loud
Whose truth
Your truth
Their truth
No truth
Defined by
Minds
perspective
The web is
Excessive
As is the drive
one finds
to feel
alive
Believe
build and reflect
Grief,

mid and id
Brain
recognitions
When pulled through
You simply regain
Reign
Liberated by
Love

Love poignant through pain

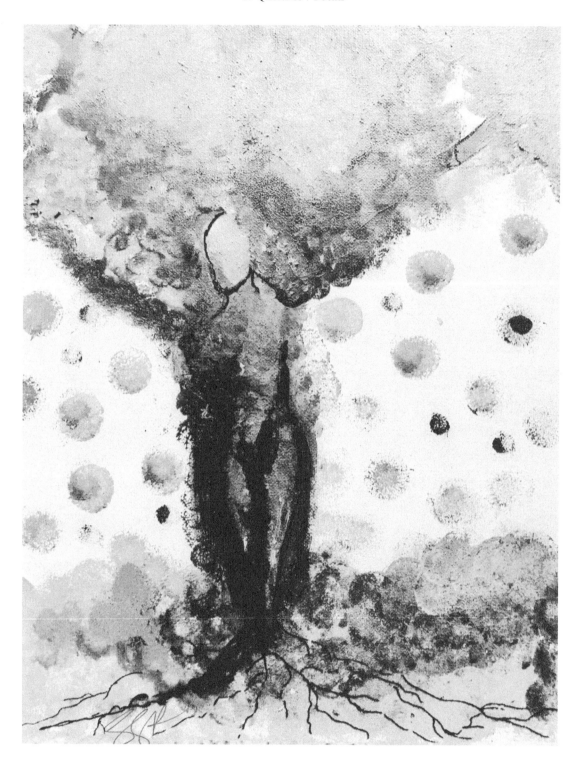

Painting by SJK "Roots"

Woods Glass Lamp

Black light
Invisible ink
Captured the hurts
Displaced
Rage
Harm and such
Dehumanization
Woods Lamp
Saw through
Cracks
Easily detected
Weaknesses
Blocked tears
Woods Lamp
Exposed
Viewed without
Protection
Woods glass diagnosed
Black
Light
Blue
Contradictions
Ahhhh...
Me too!

Woods' Lamp
Woods glass
Viewed without protection
Authenticated
Duress
Cracks are seen
Birth to the
Counterfeit
Reckless
Soul endangerment
Black light
Show it all
For on the inside
To the
Out
Woods Lamp
Woods glass
Shall show
Glow

Liberated by love
Beautiful soul

Collage of Hope by SJK

Captured community unity for freedom of SJK Sex trafficking victim incarcerated with a life without parole sentence 2012

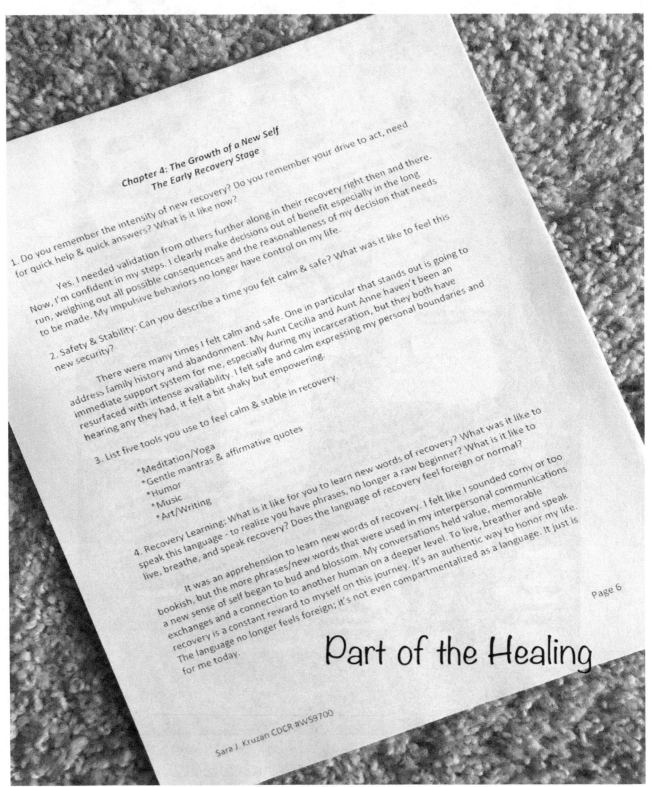

Healing 1

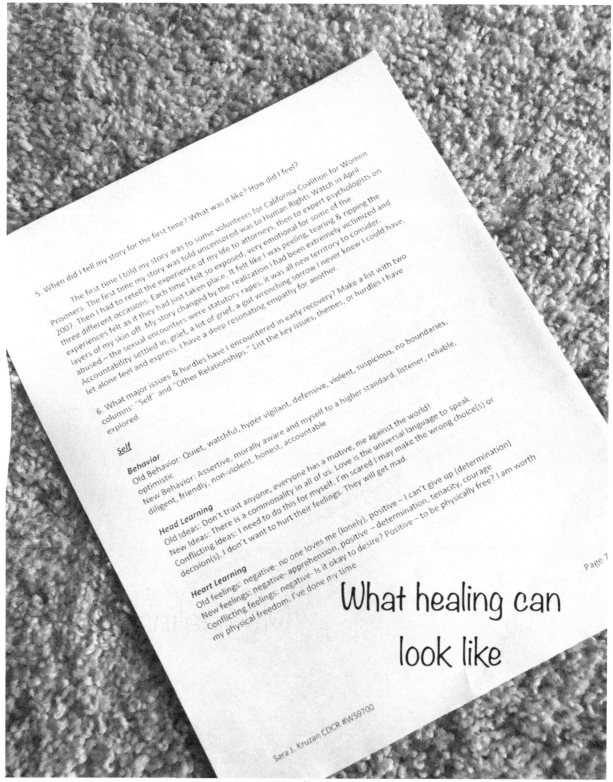

Healing 2

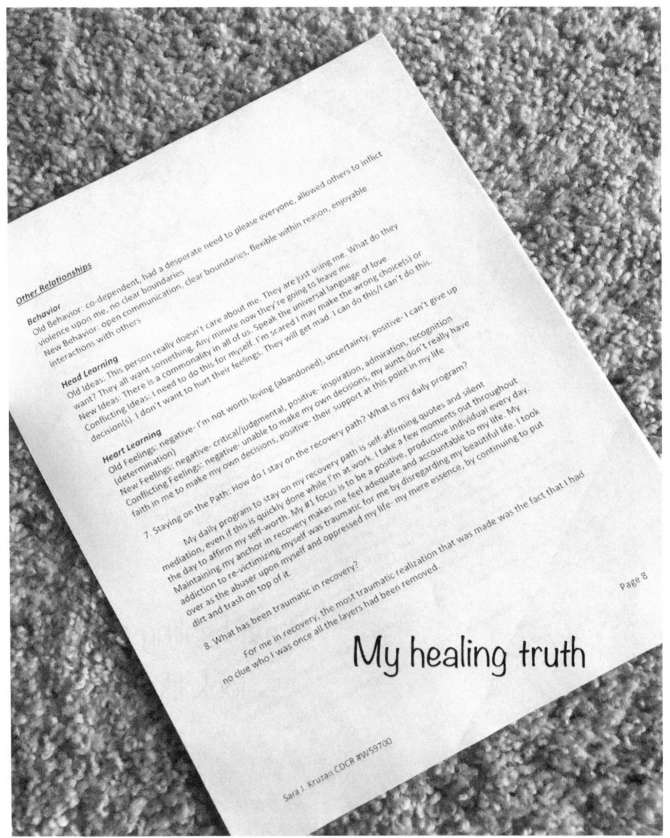

Healing 3

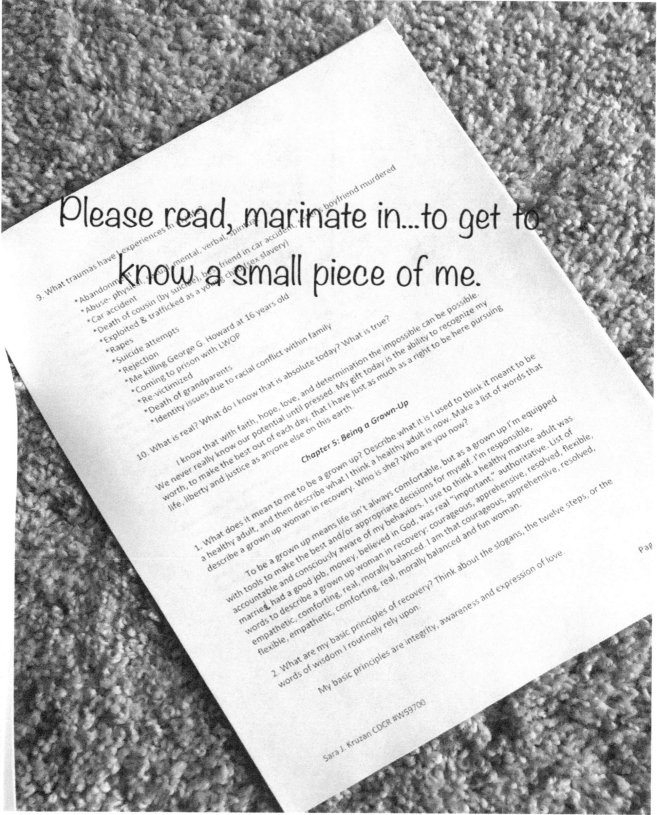

Healing 4

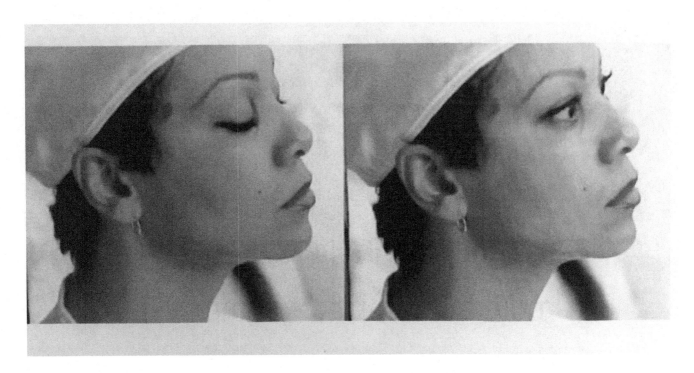

Sara Kruzan Graduation Day 2010

Jim Carson Modern Day Superhero

Artful Sunshine at Chowchilla Visiting

Showing Community Love and Support at California State Capitol

Carrie Christie Hope Agent

I.M.POSSIBLE

Through smiles with laughter, hope and encouragement are born.

Empathy and compassion, flexible understanding resides, rooted in moving

In painting, dancing, creating, and being, life explodes.

Listening and not just hearing the grief of another compels you to share in it. help in letting it go

Looking into the eyes of others without any judgment, forgiveness comes with ease.

Ice cream, butterflies, ladybugs, balloons, education- these plant the seeds of integrity.

Believing... as the impossible blooms.

These are elements that have empowered me – redefining a life rooted in strength, fueling this evolution with courage to push through. Realizing and embracing that we are not alone.

We are not only the reflection of humanity – we are the very echo etched within the wind.

It's not reasonable to believe you can control anything or anyone outside of yourself, but you do have control over thoughts, your perspective towards life, the attitude you identify with, what and how you think and what direction you take.

Be gentle with yourself; flexible and remember-we as humans reflect off one another and it is our duty to make the experience on this planet as pleasurable as possible for each other, living our greatest life ever.

Do not allow the traumas experienced to define who we are or where we want to go.

Believe in the impossible – I do every day.

Sara Kruzan

May 28, 2012

Thankful 2013

Present and intentional with beautiful souls at Los Padrinos Juvenile Hall

Bought my first car Valentine's Day 2016 Thank you Kia of Cerritos!

Living Room floor of inspiration and Hope 2018

About this author...

Far more than a survivor.

She is a simple soul.

A lifelong Friend and Advocate

Believer in Hope.

Brave, creative and such with an intentional motivation to rise above without bitter detours.

Fueled to bring Love, Justice and Dignity in a balanced manner for all deeply impacted by oppression within the California Correctional Systems.

This Author is loved deeply by a man pure and true to his soul, words and existence.

She is a mother to an ever determined, loving, empathetic energy filled essence who survived within a hostile womb.

In and with deep gratitude Sara Kruzan thanks every single person who spoke into her life.

She also sees and forgives all who have caused harm and inflicted their discretions upon her since her release from State Prison.

About Sara Kruzan...

On 10-31-2013 at 4:30 am, the song by Drake "Coming Home" came on the radio,

Sara danced with her friends, the ladies she shared an intentionally oppressive cancerous cell with...All 8 of them danced...

Liberated by hope,
In the middle of a concrete floor
in unity and purpose!

No desire for recognition, no need for a chrono to document their morals or depth of humanity...

Simply a connection etched in the innate desire to heal, connect uplift and evolve.

The tock of the clock intriguing yet a reminder

Time was falling forward,
birthing within the cinderblock
cancerous cell...
A mutation of hope and
restoration.
Sara smiles...

This author,

Sara knew, as she dressed and as she said her
"see ya laters,"

That she would be back to aide in physical liberation of others!

Sara is an active Parole Success Advocate with Uncommon Law

She is determined to create a Life Foundation to assist in restoring dignity to our fellow persons returning from incarceration.

The author believes deeply we are a reflection of one another, why not shine with Love?

For each book sold, $3.33 will be moved to a trust account established just to aide with startup funds for individuals returning into our communities

$200.00 of gate money given from the state of California to our community members returning upon their parole, is simply a disservice. Let us support with compassion filled intentions to inspire healing and just dignity and restoration.

Let's simply say,
welcome neighbor.
Let us simply ask with mindful intention...

How may I walk alongside you?

Sara, the author wishes to plant nutritious seeds, seeds which hold potential to bare fruits. Fruits to heal the wounds deep within the soul.

Thank you for sharing and holding space with this author and all who contributed to her life.

She thanks you deeply.

Please stay mindful so much more to come....

Simply,
sara

Made in the USA
Middletown, DE
22 April 2024